Contents

Snail

Silver trail
Near the kitchen door
Are there trespassers climbing
In, one with a brown whorled house
Left on our kitchen floor?

Worm

Why do you take yourself, pink fleshed and long,
On to the gritty road where vans and tractors come?

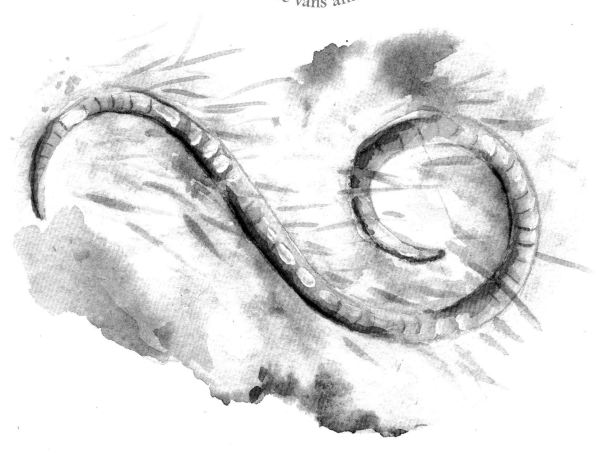

Re-routing you I feel quite pleased. But back from my walk
Meet you again. This time you're hijacked to the other bank.

Cobweb

Come and see
On the fence, traced
By the morning dew.
Who has been spinning here,
Embroidered with diamonds this
Beautiful lace, a wood nymph's shawl?

Spider

Speak to him. Take him
Prisoner (if you must) - but lift him with care.
Isn't screaming, like swooning, a fashion long
Dead? Think of him
Evicted, this eight-legged contortionist, this
Refugee.

Hamster

How would you like to spend
all of your days
Alone in your room?
My day is your night. When you
Sleep I sweat on my wheel, yearn
To tear along pipes, race through dark
Eaves, scurry with friends like
Real mice do.

White Rabbit with Yellow Flower

Their bold colour dazzles you
scattered around. Dandelions.
We pick some
for our neighbour's rabbit.
She sits in her summer doldrums.
What can a captive do
but eat?
Fetch the camera.
Let her nibble the milky stalk
in, in, in through the mesh.
Moppet poses ~ obligingly:
'White rabbit with yellow flower' .
But the netting is a pity
and somehow the wood
comes out like a cross.

Pigeon

Perhaps in the snow she had fallen exhausted
Not really injured
For in days she could perch on the twig in her box.
She grew watchful, perturbed if she sensed you were leaving.
Then   ~
A feathered explosion
Wings frantic on glass.
We carried her back to the edge of the field.
Would she rise?
With one lift she was gone.
Nice if she ever returned…stared through the window…even once.

10

Remember

in Westerham
that little robin
flying close
catching our eye
all along the old back street.
It was years and years ago ~
Some street folk's friend, perhaps,
or territorial
keeping guard.

The robin's red breast is so red
It lights up my heart and my head.
Like a secret he comes
Pecks fast the odd crumb ~
Spy Cat's gone to sleep in the shed.

Heron

He stands so still
You cannot enter his mind.
Then your heart lifts, too, as he rises
Over the stream, over the trees, over the fields.
Will the straggled wings
The reaching neck
All day
Break into your thoughts?

First published in AMBIT

Swan

Such a strange rush
in the air above
and the pulse
of the heavy wings
feels confusing.

But we know
the white bird
on its third approach,
watch it
from distance
to distance,
sense the strung nerves,
the blind search,
the awesome fear
of all love lost.

First published in AMBIT

Lapwings

She found them
Lapwings
Strayed on the road
Three nestlings
Flattening into
Merging with stone
Yet not afraid
To be lifted and held ~

Miracle~warm
New with life
Set down
With a stuck~on
Dagger beak.

Beside the verge
A fourth lay crushed
Broken
And blessed
And given.

And somewhere ~
Not far ~
A bird's unanswered
Peewit cries.

18

Owl

Out of the folding
Warmth of sleep ~ a cry that strikes ~ stops ~ then blindly
Lengthens into fear.

Bantam

Because he is Cock Robin he must, when the hutch is opened,
Always lead out. Insubordination
Needs fiery warning. Now come the courtesies.
The little hens follow.
Hilary then Polly. Is it a charade?
Attentively he beckons to the pecking ground,
Motions them towards his first discovery.
Self-sacrifice and lordly power flame in the veins of comb and
                                                                          wattle.

Luck

Bedraggled feathers are not easy
on the eye. Yet here was this little hen
being washed in a bowl, the woman
cupping her hands, spilling
the water over the bird, gently
as with a newborn child. There was no struggle.
The towel wrap, the soft blow-dry
were beauty salon pleasures. And the finished,
fluffed-up, white creation
stayed content in the holding hands. She was
keeping close to love, close to luck.

Deer

Disturbed by our presence
    near to the wooded hollow
        they raise the silent shout

Escape! The white-tailed does take off,
    veer left,
        swiftly on springs,

Effortless. But now three stags distract the eye,
    leap to the right.
        They pause mid-field,

Relax, and then, vague shadow shapes,
    with antlers lifted, fade
        into the winter trees.

My dog ~ your dog?

Does he flick you a smile
as you pass
or plead
with a long-voiced yawn
'Going to the forest?'

Do you tease your dog
with names
of famous lookalikes?
When Rocky's face gets long
and the eyes grow dark with
waiting
sometimes we say,
'Oh, poor old Abe'.

Abraham Lincoln
in history books
sits with the same grave eyes.
'Don't' you now pun,
'an thro po morph ize'
But I don't care.
I'm sure, when sad,
he feels as I might feel.

Notice how tears
begin to edge his eyes.

At last
we drive past *Greenwood Gate* ~
in minutes
Yes! *Black Hill.*
Free
he flies through the wind
bounds over bracken
over heather
chases
races with Billy
comes back
to tell us
that this
this
this
is happiness.
Ears up
no German Shepherd
moves more beautifully.

Cat

Come to our drawing room workshops. Meet
Archie. He was lost for sad months, but turned up in the ads ~
Tiger~striped guy, once mauled by a squirrel.

Cat and Mouse

Tonight the cat
played and played
with a little mouse
at the outside door,
played and played
more than I ever
watched before ~
so long I wondered
were they really ~
could they really be –
having only
a friendly game,
the cat
pawing it gently
releasing again
pawing gently
releasing again.

But look out now ~
for us ~ an offering
staining the coco mat.

Falling Asleep

She wanted a pony so badly
She wanted a pony so badly

To feed it and groom it
Right down to its hoofs

Smell the grass on its breath

Bring it in to a stable
strawed clean as a dream

whisper so …. close ….

so …. close ….

and know

all that it whispered back.

She wanted a pony so badly ….
so badly …. so badly ……

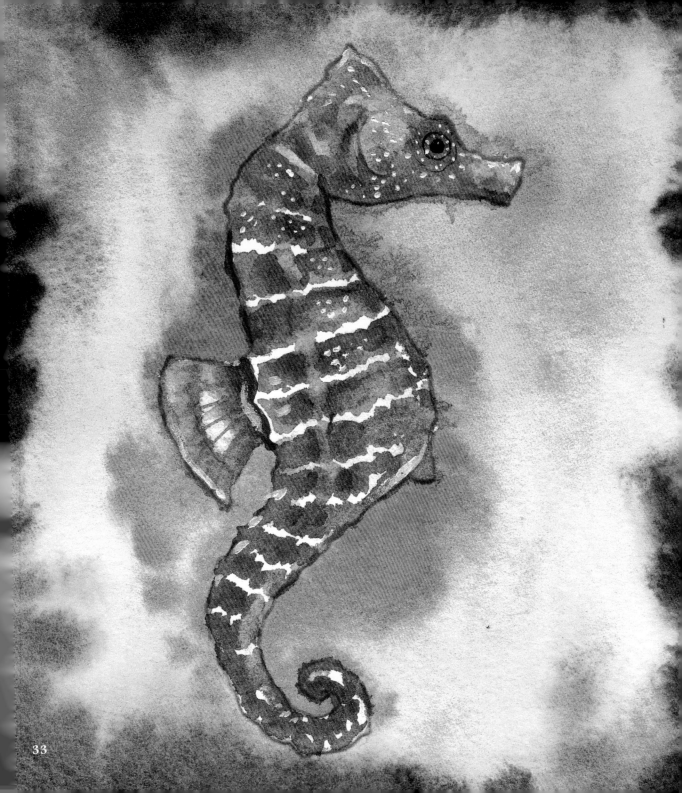

Seahorse

The little seahorse told his brother
Their father was really their mother
And he'd never fall lame
When Derby Day came
They were all of them fish - nothing other.

Little Monkey

Little climber, prankster,
acrobat on trapeze
may they not find you

grab you at play
out of tall trees

stack you at airports
numbered in boxes

manhandle you ~
motherless

keep you ~ forever ~
in quarantine

experiment on you –
laboratory clean.

Are not you,
of all creatures,
closest to me?

Bears

The polar bear paused
felt somehow, somewhere
change in the air.
Unsure in his fear
that day he walked on ~
Here was the way
bears always had gone.

Black bear
in the wilderness trees
your rich black fur
through history's years
would make one black hat
for a grenadier.

I love you, I love you, I love you
the little cub thought
stretched upside down
on the bear's curled paw.
I love you, I love you, I love you
all soft and safe and snuggly and warm.

Pansies in Flower Pot

This one standing a little unsure
in pale washed blue
is a soft voiced nurse.
Near her three laughing girls
have stepped from a plane,
sun triplets in yellow.
This pretty one loves opera,
to steal the show in purple
with no thought of growing old.
And watch the kitten eyes
in this pert face.
Is she, perhaps, a trifle cross?
Serene in velvet this one meditates,
still as a Rembrandt figure.

Burn

Why do you always call a stream
by that utterly different name? ~

Because my North has burns.
Your South has streams.

There's a worn stepping stone
at the edge of a burn
that flows under a bridge ~
a low stone bridge
that slants in a hump
near the gable end
of the house where I was born.

Goon Talk 21stC

'Have you been to the moon'
called the crocodile goon
to the glow~worm with stars in
her eyes.
'Ha, a mind~teaser question
with a time~space connection.
What is truth, clever Croc, and
what lies?

Am I weaker or stronger?
Who's been here the longer?
Have you studied your own
pedigree?'
'Come off it, old girl.
Your mind's in a whirl.
I could never invite you to tea.

But I did take a shot
Of you and your lot
with my camera one night
after dark.
The photo next day
showed the sky's Milky Way.
I expect you were one tiny spark.'

'Quick, show me the picture,'
begged the cosmic~eyed creature.
'In my dreams I've a strange
memory
of a lunar horizon
~ though there's not much to
go on ~
I might recognise one starlit sea.

Yawned the crocodile goon
'Time goes quickly to noon.
I must scrounge round for my
dinner.'
He whooshed his green tail,
threw up waves like a whale
bawled, 'Fraid I can't find your
last glimmer.'

Tag

'Let's play and have fun,'
laughed the leaves in the sun
and the crisp bag squealed in
delight.
She rose up on her toes
in the eye catching pose
of a magical cellophane kite.

'I'm coming with you.
I know what to do,'
she called as the leaves
raced ahead.
Wind rustled her dress
and she tried hard to guess
whatever it was they now said.

'You've caught us at last.
We're stupendously fast.
See, we've crossed the wide road
from Goose Green.'
'I love playing tag,'
said the breathless crisp bag.
'My address ~ can you read? ~
is Salt Dean.'

But a voice barred the way,
'We must clear these today.
Ha! a crisp bag. One more for
the boys.
They're in overdrive state,
with this book token bait,
outsmarting the ads. selling
ploys.'

The leaves didn't wait
for a composting fate.
They swirled off on a hurricane
breeze.
Their organic matter
they decided to scatter
round the roots of the
sycamore trees.

Moon

Make a fool of us still. Who wants to let go
Of the man in the moon, or the flying balloon,
Or the cow that jumped over ~ or
Nights with pearled rooftops, pining for dreams?

THE TIGER DIARIES

Nayona Nag

BlueRose ONE .co.
Stories Matter
NewDelhi • London

BLUEROSE PUBLISHERS
India | U.K.

For permissions requests or inquiries regarding this publication, please contact:

BLUEROSE PUBLISHERS
www.BlueRoseONE.com
info@bluerosepublishers.com
+91 8882 898 898
+4407342408967

ISBN: 978-93-5819-356-5

First Edition: September 2023

Dedicated to my dog Max

Introduction

Hi there! My name is Nayona, and I'm 15 years old. I want to tell you all about the most amazing creatures and places that I've been passionate about and writing on since I was 10 years old! You guessed it right - Tigers and the lush forests of India! They're like something out of a thrilling adventure story.

Tigers are just the coolest animals ever. I mean, seriously, they're like big, stripey cats, but way bigger and stronger. Did you know that they're the biggest cats in the whole wide world? And those stripes on their fur are like their own secret code – no two tigers have the same pattern. I think that's just awesome! Whenever I would see pictures of tigers, while doing my EVS project in Class 6, I imagined them as these sneaky, clever creatures, hiding in the tall grasses, waiting to surprise their prey. I would wish I could see one in real life someday. And I did! Eventually (grin).

But guess where tigers live? In these magical places called forests! And not just any forests – the incredible ones in India. There's something mysterious and exciting about those forests. The way the trees are all tall and green, and the air is so fresh – it makes me want to run and explore everything! And guess what? These forests are called "jungles" in India. I think that sounds even more exciting! Tigers are like real-life superheroes, like the kings and queens of these jungles in India. This makes them quite fascinating.

Now, let me take you on a tour of some of the coolest jungles (or as they call them in India, "jungles") where these incredible tigers live. First up, there's Ranthambore. This place is like stepping into a wild fairytale. The ancient ruins and the lush greenery make it the perfect home for tigers. I can totally imagine a tiger prowling around those old forts, just like a brave knight protecting their kingdom. I have mentioned Machli here in Tiger Diaries, she was the real Queen of Ranthambore, undisputed and magnificent in her glory days.

Then there's Jim Corbett National Park. It's like a real-life treasure trove of wildlife. Tigers, elephants, and all sorts of amazing animals call this place home. I had gone on a daring expedition, on a school trip, through the tall grasses, hoping to catch a glimpse of a majestic tiger lurking in the shadows.

Pench National Park sounds like a dream too. I heard that Rudyard Kipling's "The Jungle Book" was inspired by this very place. Can you believe that? Imagine roaming through the forests and suddenly meeting Mowgli's animal friends. It's like stepping into a storybook!

I also learned about people called "forest rangers" who help take care of these amazing jungles and the animals living there. They make sure the tigers have enough space to roam around and the other animals have a safe home too. Isn't that a fantastic job? When I went to Kanha National Reserve, in Madhya Pradesh, I went on a safari with the forest rangers and naturalists, helping to protect the tigers and their home. I even learnt how to spot animal tracks and hear the calls of the wild!

In olden times, tigers were widely hunted to a point when they were nearing extinction. I learnt, through reading, that our country did well to launch the "Save The Tiger" campaign in

India which successfully brought our national animal back from the brink of extinction. The "Save the Tiger" campaign in India still stands as a vital mission to safeguard these majestic creatures from extinction. By raising awareness, advocating for conservation, and protecting their habitats, we are writing a future where tigers continue to roam our jungles, enriching our planet's biodiversity and cultural heritage. Also now, we have to focus on the increasing human- wildlife conflicts in reserve areas.

So, there you have it – my fascination with tigers and the enchanting Indian forests, which I have captured in my Tiger Diaries as I can spent the best years of my middle school life poking around in the school library, reading, looking at pictures, scrounging the school newspapers for articles on famous tigers like Collarwali, Avni, Zalim T-25 and dreaming about the day I shall see a real tiger in a real jungle. Until then, I decided to journal all the incredible adventures waiting for me among the tall trees and hidden paths of India's magical jungles.

Dear Reader, I welcome you to read my Tiger Diaries - the diary of a little girl fascinated with the Tiger, her journey, trials and travails as she documents her passion, from 6th to 8th grade, in a little diary with newspaper cuttings and smoking hot commentary on her day-to-day shenanigans tracking the magnificent beast, for other young readers to read, laugh and wonder and feel incredulously impassioned just as she is about The Royal Bengal Tiger! ROAR!

Nayona Nag

Tiger Aficionado and Author

this is what I found today.
An article on a tiger saved
in a shop*! I was so glad
As they put the tiger in a
rehabilation centre to free it
instead of killing it. I think
they had some empathy for
the tiger being stuck for
about three days. I am
also going to adopt a tiger
in the Ranthambore Tiger
Reserve. I have been there
before to get a sighting
of a tigeress called Thil
with my cousin-sister
Richa who lives in U.S.A.
I have also been to
Jim Corbett National Reserve
with my friends for a
school trip and I got a
sighting of a tiger at 3 am
near the swimming pool)

November 21st, 2018.

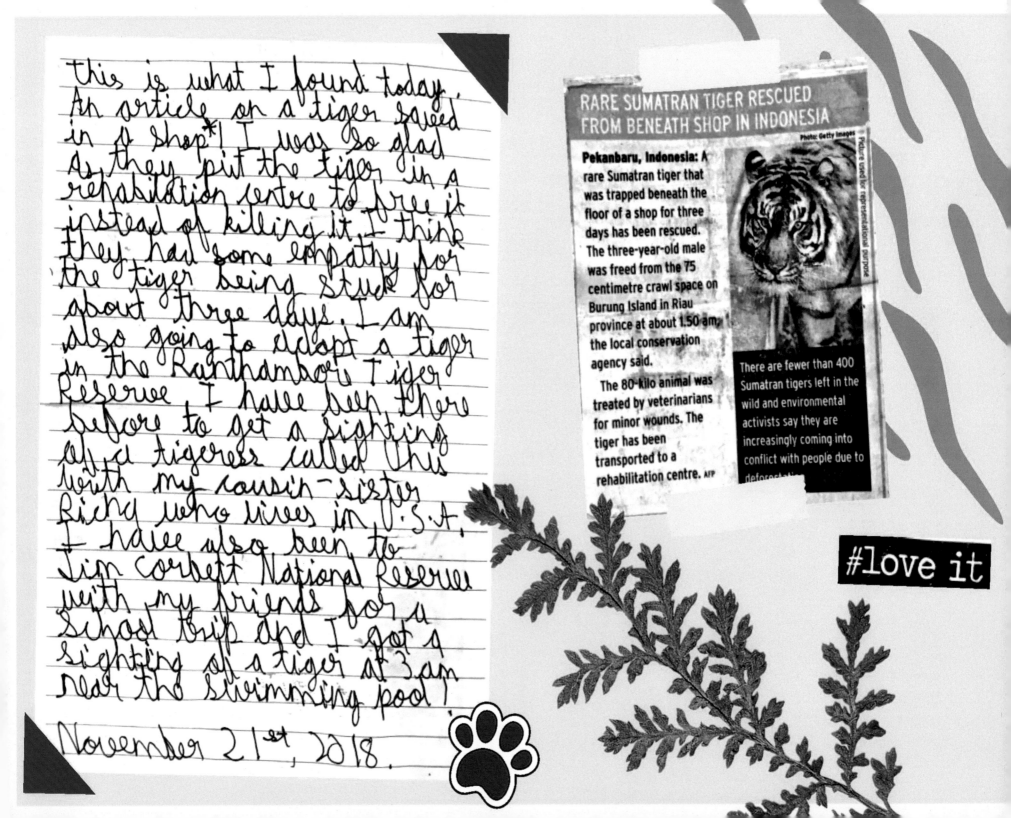

RARE SUMATRAN TIGER RESCUED FROM BENEATH SHOP IN INDONESIA

Photo: Getty images

Pekanbaru, Indonesia: A rare Sumatran tiger that was trapped beneath the floor of a shop for three days has been rescued. The three-year-old male was freed from the 75 centimetre crawl space on Burung Island in Riau province at about 1.50 am, the local conservation agency said.

The 80-kilo animal was treated by veterinarians for minor wounds. The tiger has been transported to a rehabilitation centre. AFP

There are fewer than 400 Sumatran tigers left in the wild and environmental activists say they are increasingly coming into conflict with people due to deforestation

Picture used for representational purpose

#love it

RARE SUMATRAN TIGER GIVES BIRTH TO FOUR CUBS

The female Sumatran tiger Mayang's four cubs made an appearance in their enclosure at Berlin's Tierpark zoo. Mayang gave birth to four cubs, two male, two female, named Willi, Oscar, Seri and Kiara. The Sumatran tiger is a rare tiger subspecies that inhabits the Indonesian island of Sumatra and is classified as critically endangered with between 350 to 450 individuals left. REUTERS

ADORABLE

Finally after a million days, an article has come out on the tigers. For now this is the cutest article. A rare Sumatran tiger gave birth to four cubs. Their names are Willi, Oscar, Seri and Kiara. The name of the tiger who gave birth was called Mayang. My favourite cub is Oscar as he is a bit jumpy. I am also planning a birthday party on the topic tigers and I will paste the best picture in the diary. What else could be better. The day is starting to become good already. This time, the next article of tigers should better come early, not late.

4th December, 2018.

So it is just one more day till Christmas and it has been a month since I have got a tiger article so my mom got a printout of three articles. They are kind of white which kind of changes the pattern but it's okay. This is good as Royal Bengal Tigers have been spotted in three locations of Odisha! As in my first article, their are 25 to 30 royal Bengal Tigers left. They have kept three of them safe. The locations are Hemagiri forest in Sudargarh, Debrigad Wildlife Century in Hirakud and Muniguda in Rayagada district. God knows what I am gonna get for Christmas. I hope it is something related to tigers.

December 24th 2018

THE TIMES OF INDIA

Royal Bengal Tigers spotted in three new locations in Odisha

PTI | Sep 30, 2018, 10.34 AM IST

BHUBANESWAR: The Odisha government has said that Royal Bengal Tigers (RBTs) have been spotted in three new locations in the state.

Forest and environment minister, Bijayshree Routray said on Saturday that RBTs "presence have been reported" from Hemgiri forest in Sundargarh, Debrigad Wildlife Century in Hirakud and Muniguda in Rayagada district.

The minister said the presence of the RBTs have been confirmed from pictures captured in cameras installed in the forests.

"There should be around 60 RBTs in Odisha. However, they were not earlier sighted at these three places. Tiger being found in Muniguda of Rayagada district is definitely a good news," said Routray.

The official count as per the 2014 census is 40 tigers in Odisha, said Sandip Tripathy, the Principal Chief Conservator of Forests (Wild Life) adding that the current census by NTCA (national tiger conservation authority), Wildlife Institute of India (WII) and Odisha Forest Department is underway.

"Ther result of the current tiger census will be available early next year," Tripathy said.

Meanwhile, the minister said the Forest department has been instructed to take steps to ensure safety of the tigers and maintain their habitation.

"Our forests have huge potential and the population of Royal Bengal Tigers will definitely increase in future," the minister said.

The Centre and the state government had earlier a dispute over the tiger population in Odisha. Citing a 2016 report, the Centre had said that the state had 28 Royal Bengal Tigers, while the Odisha government claimed to be home to 40 RBTs and 318 leopards.

The tiger census report of the state government was also rejected by the NTCA, which had put the number of big cats at 28.

The counting of RBTs was done only in Shimilipal and Satkosia Tiger Reserves and could not be held in other places during 2016, Forest officials said.

SAVE TIGERS NOW!

The only bad article that I recieved was the first one. The news had become from good to bad. Maharastra loses 16 tigers in 11 months! One of them I already know from start is Avni. The other 15 to me are is unknown. I am so upset as they died in a tiger reserve. Now as I know that there is a tiger reserve in Maharastra I am sonna kill then literlay kill them! I want more tigers to come or migrate to this place as this is a catostrophere before Christmas. I hope there are no hunters on the lose on Christmas Eve.

December 24th, 2018

Maharashtra loses 16 tigers in 11 months

TNN | Nov 25, 2018, 12:15 AM IST

PUNE: Sixteen tigers, including five cubs, have died this year so far in Maharashtra, data from the National Tiger Conservation Authority's (NTCA) indicates.

The deaths also include T1 or Avni in Pandharkawade and the three cubs crushed on the railway tracks in Chandrapur in November.

STATE LOSES 5 CUBS IN 11 MONTHS

DEATHS IN MAHA	
2018 (Till Nov 11)	16
2017	21
2016	16
2015	12
2014	7
2013	10
2012	13

Locations | **Pandharkawda** | FDCM, Chandrapur, Junona Range | Sindewahi Range, **Brahmapuri** | **Pench** | Talodhi Range, **Brahmapuri** | Pench, Kolitmara, **West Pench Range** | Talodhi Range, **Chandrapur** | FDCM, Chandrapur Junona Range | Pench, MP | Maharashtra border, Piwarthadi and others

Tiger deaths have been the highest in the last three years since 2012 with 21 in 2017 and 16 in 2016. The state was second in the number of tiger deaths this year after Madhya Pradesh.

As many as 12 of the 16 deaths this year were outside the tiger reserve. Experts attributed the deaths to humans killing tigers moving outside the protected area out of fear or tigers dying in road or rail accidents.

Ten of the 16 deaths were under the 'details awaited' category as the cause of deaths in the database. The reason for the three cubs crushed under a train in the Chandrapur Junona range earlier this month was attributed to 'unnatural' causes, while that of a cub in Pench was put as infighting.

Some deaths occurred outside the tiger reserve where humans may have killed the animal straying out of the reserve, Rajesh Gopal, secretary general, Global Tiger Forum and a former head of NTCA, told TOI.

"In tiger landscapes, a large number of natural deaths also happen due to infighting, which is healthy. Deaths outside the reserves are unhealthy. Once tigers have space in a reserve, their sociology also requires that they get a bit of space outside the reserve via tiger corridors to move about," he said.

Tiger corridors encroached upon by people create conflict. "A tiger entering such spaces then becomes a nuisance. The animal is killed outside a reserve because humans view it as a threat or want to keep it away from cattle," Gopal added.

Senior wildlife veterinarian and forensic expert from KVAFSU Karnataka, Prayag HS, said natural deaths of tigers is normal. "The railway tracks' death of the cubs was avoidable. Electrocution remains one of the various threats that tigers in Maharashtra are exposed to. Development also causes loss of wild animals. A balance between conservation and development is necessary," Prayag said.

OMG

'Satkosia littered with metal snares'

TNN | Nov 18, 2018, 10.50 AM IST

BHUBANESWAR: Wildlife experts suspect that thousands of snares, placed by poachers to hunt prey animals, are currently strewn across Satkosia Tiger Reserve. While the autopsy report of male tiger MB2 — who died within four months of being brought to the state from Madhya Pradesh's Kanha Tiger Reserve — is yet to be published, the injury on his neck is believed to have been caused by a metal trap of the kind poachers use in the area.

Local poachers use wires made of rust-proof iron to build the traps. They also use the cables of motorcycle brakes, as these are very strong. "The wires are fixed across several bamboo sticks, which are arranged in a way so as to withstand the resistance of the animal and create a tight grip," said a wildlife officer.

"The more the animal struggles to escape the trap, the more severe is the injury. Most of the animals remain entrapped and finally die of their wounds as well as hunger. Only in rare cases does the animal escape," said a wildlife officer.

Poachers place the snares in areas frequented by prey animals such as wild boar, sambar and deer, and then leave. "A trap in which an animal has been snared becomes useless," he added. The poachers observe the movement of animals, especially herbivores, for days before planting the snares.

A forest officer said the only way to detect wire-laden entrapments was to use metal detectors. Traps can activate the signal on a detector from a minimum of 50 meters and a maximum of 100 meters. "The forest field personnel should use hand-held metal detectors while walking along animal paths," said wildlife campaigner Biswajit Mohanty.

MB2's carcass bore a deep injury on the dorsal region of the neck. When the carcass was found on Wednesday, the wound was maggot-infested and was believed to be five days old.

Meanwhile, the team of wildlife experts from the Wildlife Institute of India and the National Tiger Conservation Authority (NTCA), which visited the site where MB2 was found dead, returned after taking note of the circumstances leading to the death of the animal. It will file a report soon. The team comprised WII scientist K Ramesh, who has been overseeing the tiger translocation project in the state since the beginning, and inspector general (NTCA) Amit Mallik.

Are you kidding me?!. One more day till Kristmas and things are already becoming worse. Satkosia littered with metal snares is the article. One of the male tigers died as the river was flooded with things like metal. As if there are many tiger activists in Delhi so I wanted to join one. I heard that also in reserves that I have found the visitors throw garbage, water bottles and try to feed them! This is annoying as two cubs where surrounded by seven jeeps and the visitors are like, "Here, Kitty Kitty." Some of them throw bottles to see how their reaction is like. The tigers get so scared.

December 24th, 2018

I don't really understand this article that quiet much but I do understand that it's about roads or something, I really think that the tigers in the article look so cute! I may be overdoing as that is what I did on the 3rd page.* I think the article is about these road projects threatening the existence of tigers. I don't know how but somehow it does. Well my tiger party is coming out to be awesome as I am turning it... and on the next page, it is gonna be alot of fun. turn on the next page now! So..... *Drumroll* →

December 24th, 2018

Reinforce rules in tiger corridors, buffer zones: NTCA

TNN | Nov 30, 2018, 06.04 AM IST

NAGPUR: Realising that projects like roads, railways and powers lines are proving detrimental for tigers, the National Tiger Conservation Authority (NTCA) has directed all chief wildlife wardens (CWLWs) in tiger-ranging states to strongly comply with existing statutory provisions of the Wildlife Protection Act. The circular was issued on Wednesday.

Taking serious note of the recent reports in TOI, the NTCA on November 28 asked chief wildlife wardens to assert on Section 38(O)(1)(b) of the Wildlife Protection Act, 1972 which says: "Evaluate and assess various aspects of sustainable ecology and disallow any ecologically unsustainable and use such as, mining, industry and other projects within the tiger reserve."

It also asked wardens to maintain another clause of the same section, which says: "Ensure that the tiger reserves and areas linking one protected area or tiger reserve with another protected area or tiger reserve are not diverted for ecologically unsustainable uses, except in public interest and with the approval of the National Board for Wildlife (NBWL) and on the advice of the NTCA."

Both, NTCA, the topmost authority monitoring tiger reserves, and CWLWs are being ignored while implementing these infrastructure projects. A CWLW is the deciding authority in every state on wildlife matters.

TOI had recently reported that Maharashtra CWLW was bypassed while planning road development projects in corridor and buffer of six tiger reserves in Vidarbha.

Earlier, as reported by TOI on July 29, of the 1,697 road, irrigation and railway projects, 399 projects worth Rs1.3 lakh crore are coming up in the tiger landscape of Central India and Eastern Ghats. Spread over eight states, the area is home to 688 (31%) of the country's 2,226 tigers and these projects threaten the existence of the big cats.

The most awesome page.
Merry Christmas to all!!!
I hope the new year improves
for the life of the tigers.
These are my Christmas
presents! That is me in the
picture (obviously). I got a
cute stuff tiger as I forgot
to write Santa a letter, so I
wrote one before Christmas.
So I told Santa that I
don't want a gift but a wish
to be fulfilled and that wish
was to save the tigers. Santa
gave me the tiger. I called
the tiger Unis. The tiger I saw
in Ranthambore. My other two
tigers are Simba and Aeni.
Simba siberian and Aeni normal.
I got a bottle, tiffin and fox.
So a Merry Christmas again.

Christmas

I am in U.S.A, California and
I am writing this at night.
I went to the National Museum
of Science Academics. Their where
penguins, reefs, rays, snakes and
even anacondas and sharks! I was
passing the dinosaur gallery
with my cousin-sister Richa;
when I saw this*. A panthera
tiger statue. There was an X-
ray where there were pics
of tigers changing. They are
found in the rainforest as
in the rainforest it was
mentioned. I don't really know
why they are not mentioned in
the article of Page no. 1. I guess
this species of tigers are very
rare and so that hunters don't
know about this. So... Happy New
Year once again.

December 31st 2018

AWESOME

Happy New Year!

FUN

OMG!! I am in paradise! These are the pics of my birthday party in the trampoline park! I had so much fun! Eleen if I almost broke my nose in the foam pit. The cake looks gourgeous and awesome. It was amazing to taste with the chocolate inside. I also had nuggets, oreo milkshake with pizza. My friends made it even more interesting by playing the old musical chairs. We would jump and jump and jump till we get sick. We played basketball, wrestled and were swinging on ropes in the air with rock climbing. I had so much fun and these pictures will or shall never fade away.

January 27ᵗʰ, 2019

OK, OK OK! I have had a wonderful day today and yesterday. My best friend in the world Gayatri is a fan of tigers like me. Sooo I am work-ing with her and making posters in a sleepover! I have gotten 2 articles today! One was very long so they are in the other page. The first art-icle is about a tiger and the lion and they are mixed species! The name of these species are Tigon and a Liger. This is an interesting valentines day News. The image of the tiger is very very like My Christmas stuffed toy this! It is yellow. The image is on the next page so lets take a look sooo....... *Drumroll* →

Valentines Day

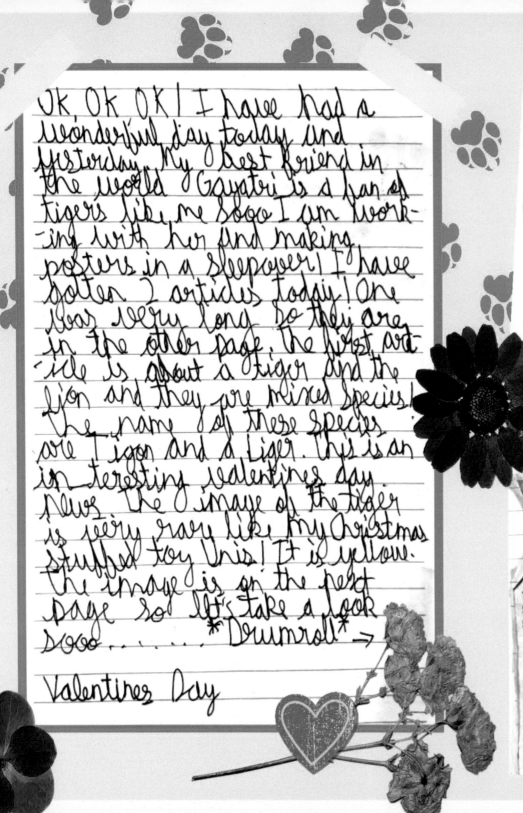

WHAT IS A **TIGON** AND **A LIGER?**

SUNIL DHAVALA

AMALA: Hello! Nat Geo uncle, What is a tigon and a liger?

NAT GEO UNCLE (NGU): A tigon is a hybrid cat that results from the cross-breeding of a male tiger and a female lion (lioness). A liger is a crossbreeding of a male lion and a female tiger (tigress).

AAKIFAH: Do lions and tigers co-exist?
NGU: In the jungle, tigers and lions do not usually meet. They are two different species; usually live in different habitats, regions and continents. Tigers are native to Asia whereas the majority of the lions live in Africa.

AAKIFAH: Why do humans create these crossbreeds, is there any purpose?
NGU: Private zookeepers and circus compa-nies breed tigons and ligers as a special attraction in order to attract more audiences.

AGNES: What are the main characteristic of the tigons and ligers? Are they endangered?
NGU: Ligers are the largest among big cats. Their weight is as much as a tiger and lion put together. Tigons, on the other hand, weigh half of a liger's weight. Tigons can have spots or stripes. They roar like lions and growl like tigers. Scientists do not consider them as natural species. Their population is minimal.

AMALA: Are they healthy and happy?
NGU: Since tigers are solitary and lions are social, their offspring exhibit conflicting behavioural characteristics, they develop hyper-aggression and depression. Most of the hybrids are prone to deafness, blind-ness and are born with weak hearts owing to their mismatched genes. They usually have short life spans.

AGNES: What happens to the second generation of these hybrids?
NGU: The second-generation hybrid of a female liger and lion is called a lilige. The litigon is a second-generation hybrid of female tigon and lion. The titigon is a second-generation hybrid of female tigon and tiger.

NGU: Do you know that there is only one place in the world where tigers coexist with lions?
Agnes, Aakifah and Amala in chorus: "Gi[r] National Forest in Gujarat."

NGU: Correct! Thanks kids, for joining. let's invite Amar, Akbar and Anthony next time to talk about snakes.
(WRITER IS QUIZMASTER, COLUMNIST, AUTHOR, SPEAKER, PANELIST AND EDUCATOR. HAD SPENT A DECADE WITH NATIONAL GEOGRAPHIC, ALSO HELD SENIOR MANAGEMENT ROLES AT RADIO TELEVISION LUXEMBOURG ETC)

LEARNING WITH TIMES NIE

Nat Geo Uncle is here to break it down for Amala, Akifah, Agnes and You...

XOXO

Climate change could wipe out Bengal tigers

ALERT

Sundarbans — the iconic Bengal tiger's last coastal stronghold and the world's biggest mangrove forest — could be destroyed by climate change and rising sea levels over the next 50 years, scientists say. "Fewer than 4,000 Bengal tigers are alive today," said Bill Laurance, a professor at the James Cook University, Australia. "That's a really low number for the world's biggest cat, which used to be far more abundant but today it is mainly confined to small areas of India and Bangladesh," Laurance said.

The Sundarbans region of Bangladesh and India, the biggest mangrove forest on Earth, is also the most critical area for the Bengal tiger

The first image is this tiger! The stripes are very hardly visible as they are half-lion. I think this species of tigers are barely found so I can't spot one. My science teacher Ma'am Garima just now went to Sariska National Park and a tiger was following her! I can try to spot these species. Anyway, this is bad News. All because climate change Bengal Tigers will wipe out! Already there was an alert that Bengal tigers are already going to be extinct in the end of the century so what else! I am making 3 youtube channels and one of them is about tigers. I need to warn Gayatri about this.

Valentines Day

14 FEB

This time it is a bit weird. It randomly appeared. Today was open day about I had to do activities. I was racing when suddenly a paper appeared and it was on tigers. I was stunned as I think it was part of 15th grade student. I took it home and copied it. The paper I found was torn. Anyways I am going to give it back to someone. I was so happy as whoever wrote this was amazing! He/She was too working on tigers. I also got a sticker is a Spanish activity on a tiger[*] I am also down with Nia, after sport-hunting yesterday. I may not go to school but I hope I don't miss an article.

February 17th, 2019

Save the tiger before they are silenced forever.

Save the national animals and serve the nation

Keep calm and Save the tigers

Look at the tigers
Mighty and strong
Killing them
for their skin
is very wrong

Save our Tigers
Save our pride

Mighty tigers, hear them roar
For they may be no more

Fight for the right of the Tigers

Killing tigers is the greed not the need

Save our striped friends

Don't be wild to the tiger, help save them!
Save a tiger, Save a life.

OH SNAP

MARCH 6, 2019 | VOL. 1

Read More About Tigers Around the World: www.bit.ly/211tiger.info

Endangered Amur Tiger Cubs Born at Dublin Zoo

ENVIRONMENT

Dublin Zoo, located in the capital city of Ireland, recently announced the birth of two endangered female Amur tiger cubs to first time parents, Tundra and Ussuri. According to the zoo, the cubs weighed about 1.6kgs each at the time of birth and have now become a healthy 15kgs each. Reports state that only 9,000 Amur tigers have been counted in the wild.

DID YOU KNOW?
Amur tigers are also known as Siberian tigers.

Niccee

My gosh! A million years it has been since I have gotten an article. Number one the newspaper monitor is always forgetting to get the newspapers. So my trustworthy best friend Mehak had a whole newspaper on tigers! So she got me this article which came in handy. An endangered Amur tiger gave birth to cubs in a zoo. I couldn't read the article that quite much as it was blurry and torn. But all I understand is that the cub and Mom are in critical danger. I just came back from Jaipur and I heard that I shall be going to Sariska next week! I am so excited and I hope I get a tiger.

March 6th, 2019

It has been ages since I got an article. This is not really one but it suits. This is on Earth Day. A tiger is in both articles. And check out my new series of journals called "The Ghosthunters" with Zanna, Kaniskha and Gayatri. It is about a ghost that killed my dog called Nawab and the spirits name is Samaira and we are trying to hunt her down. I am relieved that an article has come. I am so mad at the newspaper monitor Shaurya B. I am finally in class 7 and we all are shuffled. So I hope something good happens this year. I have found 7 new tiger reserves that I shall obviously go to all of them. And I got a new dog called Max.

April 24th, 2019

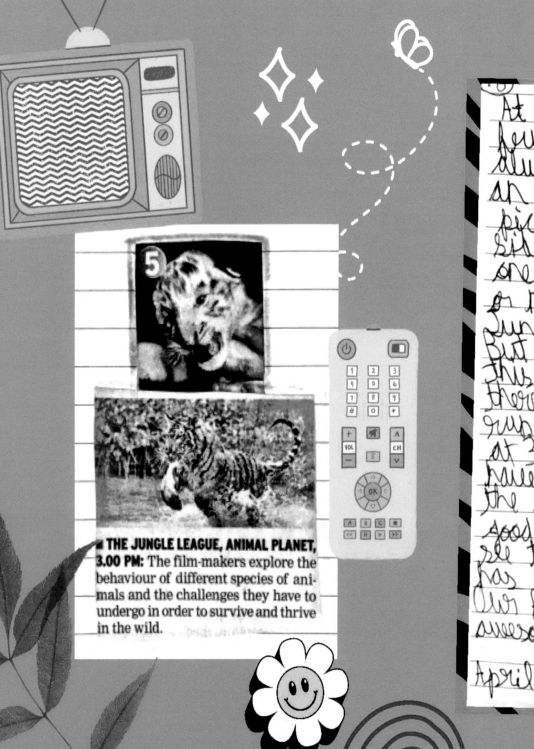

THE JUNGLE LEAGUE, ANIMAL PLANET, 3.00 PM: The film-makers explore the behaviour of different species of animals and the challenges they have to undergo in order to survive and thrive in the wild.

At least I have got just a few articles that works. Like always this is not really an article. I found a picture of an liger, a white siberian tiger and. The other one is where we or I am or may see this movie called Jungle league (Not justice league). But I don't think I can as this stupid BSF function is there but I am going to run away from the school at 3 for swimming. But I have to tell my mom to record the movie. I hope this goes good. I recomend you all to see this movie. Also Netflix has released a show called Our planet which is totally awesome on Tigers.

April 30th, 2019

I think it has been 15 days since I got an articles but today JACKPOT! 4 articles in a day! I was stumped. I lost 2 teeth last night and I told the tooth fairy to give me some articles and it came! I got these 3 articles in a newspaper, but in the library, I found another! So I am apparently bunking library period but it's worth it. I am actually so happy and this is going to be 4 pages long. I am a bit worried as the Bengal tigers or the Sunderbans are in grave danger because of climate change. But thanks to my science teacher, we are doing a project of climate change after the holidays which is dayafter tomorrow.

May 15ᵗʰ, 2019

be Yourself

BENGAL TI
MAY NOT SURVIVE
CLIMATE CHANGE
Climate change and rising sea levels may eventually wipe out one of world's last and lar...

RAISE HANDS FOR THE ENVIRONMENT

The cats are among nearly 500,000 land species whose survival is in question because of threats to their natural habitats, according to a United Nations report.

The Sundarbans, 4,000 square miles of marshland in Bangladesh and India, hosts the world's largest mangrove forest and a rich ecosystem supporting several hundred animal species, including the endangered Bengal tiger.

But 70% of the land is just a few feet above sea level, and grave changes are in store for the region, Australian and Bangladeshi researchers reported in the journal 'Science of The Total Environment'. Changes wrought by a warming planet will be 'enough to decimate' the few hundred or so Bengal tigers remaining there. "By 2070, there will be no suitable tiger habitats remaining in the Bangladesh Sundarbans," concluded the study by 10 researchers.

The paper, which relies on climate scenarios developed by the Intergovern-mental Panel on Climate Change simulation models, adds to existing studies that offered similarly grim predictions for wildlife in the Sundarbans.

Sharif A Mukul, lead author of the new report on the Sundarbans, and his colleagues looked for risks to the tiger beyond sea level rise, which accounted for 5.4% to 11.3% of the projected habitat loss in 2050 and 2070. Other factors related to climate change were more damaging to the Sundarbans' tigers, one of the largest remaining populations of wild tigers in the world, the researchers found. Since the early 1900s, habitat loss, hunting and the illegal trade of animal parts have decimated the global population of tigers from around 100,000 to fewer than 4,000.

In the Bangladesh Sundarbans, a spike in extreme weather events and changing vegetation will further reduce the population, the study found. And as the Sundarbans flood, confrontations may grow between humans and tigers as the animals stray outside their habitat in search of new land. "A lot of things might

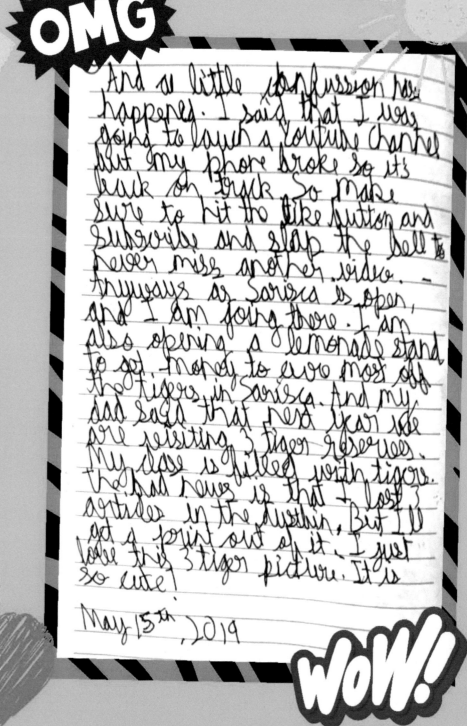

And a little confussion has happened. I said that I was going to layer a youtube chantel but my phone broke so it's back on Truck. So make sure to hit the like button and subscribe and slap the bell to never miss another video. Anyways as Sariska is open, and I am going there. I am also opening a lemonade stand to get money to save most of the tigers in Sariska. And my dad said that next year we are visiting 3 tiger reserves. My close is filled with tigers. The bad news is that I lost 3 artiles in the Austin. But I'll get a print out of it. I just love this 3 tiger picture. It is so cute!

May 15th, 2019

So I hope something goes good as last year. Anyways today is the last day of school. So I am happy happy and sad sad. I am happy because I am able to enjoy my summer holidays, but the bad news is the I'm gonna miss my friends, ghost-hunting and worse. No more tiger articles! So I am going to kind of stop writing and focus more on my channel. I can write if Nehak gives me more articles! (She's better). So I am at August 15th going to Sariska after the summer vacation do it's perfect weather for a tiger to be roaming about. One of my aunts went to Ranthambore and saw 7 tigers in one day!!

May 17th, 2019

TIGER

TIGER COUNT ON INDIAN SIDE OF SUNDERBANS SET TO RISE

Indian Sunderbans is set to post a handsome growth in tiger numbers in the national report likely to be released next month.

If the initial trend in the analysis made by the state forest department is to be believed, at least 94 big cats were photographed in the mangroves, including the tiger reserve and South 24 Parganas forest division areas, during the camera-trap exercise for 2018. The count was 87 in 2016-17. State foresters are yet to go official about the number because the final data, to be compiled by Dehradun-based Wildlife Institute of India (WII), will be arrived at after using refined technology that will eliminate possibilities of the same animals being counted twice. A senior state forest official said they expected an upper limit of 110 tigers on the Indian side of Sunderbans. IANS

happen," said Mukul, an assistant professor of environmental management at Independent University, Bangladesh in Dhaka. "The situation could be even worse if there is a cyclone or if there is some disease outbreak in that area, or a food shortage."

In October, a landmark report by the United Nations' scientific panel on climate change found that if greenhouse gas emissions continued at the current rate, the atmosphere would warm as much as 2.7 degrees Fahrenheit above preindustrial levels by 2040.

That increase would have significant consequences for food chains, coral reefs and flood-prone areas. It may also disproportionally affect poorer, densely packed countries like Bangladesh, which is about the size of Iowa and home to 160 million people.

In an analysis of decades of tidal records, scientists found that high tides were rising much faster than the global average in Bangladesh, which sits in the Ganges Delta, a complex network of rivers and streams.

Sugata Hazra, an oceanographer at India's Jadavpur University, said there may be some loss of land in the Sunderbans, but his research suggested a less dramatic impact on tigers. Some steps have been taken to protect low-lying areas and the tigers living there, said Zahir-uddin Ahmed, an official with Bangladesh's forest department. NYT

feast your eyes

CORBETT'S STAR ATTRACTIONS

Two graceful big cats aged 9 to 10 years, with their three cubs, are providing delight to droves of tourists at the Jim Corbett Tiger Reserve in Uttarakhand. "Both the tigresses aren't shy and walk with the cubs even when tourists are around. Sightseers who spot them leave immensely satisfied and those who don't, vow to return again," a guide said. For the detailed report, go to >P2

PHOTO CREDIT: PV & SARITA SUBRAMANIAM

AMAZING

So this picture is the greatest of all! I found this in the library. Corbett's populations are getting pretty high. Even if I saw this in my pad the tiger kind of looks like me and sister Risha. I am surprised that they aren't so shy. And sorry for the nonsense on the page. I blame all the boys fault. So some people have been asking me how do you catch a tiger sighting during a safari. So all you need to do is select the best track with the most number of tigers. They go near a place full of deer. Then you wait till a call from the deer comes. A call is a sign of danger that a tiger

May 17th, 2019

(23)

Is coming. So if you are patient enough, then you can get a sighting. But you need to be really quiet and patient. And pls don't jump out of the jeep to touch the tiger. Impatient people, beware. So I guess this article is about tigers cooling them selfes by swimming in a pool of algae to save itself from climate change. Also I yesterday went to a weather report station and I wore a tiger cap. No offense but it looked like a bears on my head and it looked quite ugly on me. And also my sister's mom have come to our home to play. So Happy Summer Holidays!!!

May 17th, 2019

Photo: PTI

A white tiger cools itself in a pond at its enclosure as temperatures soar at Alipore ZoologicalGardens, in Kolkata, recently

PICTURE OF THE WEEK

PM RELEASES TIGER CENSUS REPORT

THE TIGER ROARS AGAIN!

INTERNATIONAL TIGER DAY

Prime Minister Narendra Modi on Monday released the All India Tiger Estimation Report 2018 and said the country has emerged as one of the biggest and safest habitats for tigers in the world. "With around 3,000 tigers, India has emerged as of one of the biggest and safest habitats for them in world," Modi said as he lauded all the stakeholders involved in the country's tiger conservation exercise. "Nine long years ago, it was decided in St. Petersburg (Russia) that the target of doubling the tiger population would be 2022. We, in India, completed this target four years in advance. This is the finest example of Sankalp Se Siddhi (Attainment through Resolve)," he said. The story of protecting tigers that started with 'Ek Tha Tiger' (there was once a tiger) and reached 'Tiger Zinda Hai' (the tiger is alive) should not end there. Efforts towards conservation should be expanded and sped up, he added.

The tiger population in the country has grown from 1,400 in 2014 to 2,977 in 2019, according to the report

■ **TIGERLAND, ANIMAL PLANET, 3.00 PM:** Project CAT reveals how it plans to prevent the extinction of tigers, one of the planet's most endangered animals, by doubling their population in the wild by 2022.

20th century around 95% of the global tiger population has been lost

4 Tigers are considered as an 'Umbrella Species' - their conservation also protects many other species

---

Hey, so the holidays have ended and I had a long break but now as I am back to school in July I am glad to announce that "International Tigers Day" has arrived!! Look at these two articles that I found in today's newspaper just awaiting for me. One is obviously on the great celebration of the Tiger where the tiger population has actually increased by quite a lot, I've been told that 33% of the population has increased!! I am so fortunate that the Indian government has worked hard to achieve this. With that comes a second article, on "Project CAT"? It's a show on TV! And it shows the plans to help tigers! Wow I wish I could bunk half of school and watch it but sadly school has it 2:15pm.ish. But I'M STILL HAPPY as today is a great day.
July 30th, 2019.

It's almost been a month of. But it's alright as I have gone two months without an article before. Lot. But luckily it was worth wanting as this article is a good one. There are MORE increase in tigers. Yes. Ever since Tiger Day has passed good news it has been too. Now from 33% it is now 75%. That's a huge increase! The tigers have started growing and they are facing their problems with pride. It is also a victory for India, our nation. The tiger reserves have done well and put effort. Speaking of tiger reserves, another thing mentioned in the article, a tiger reserve called "Periyar Tiger Reserve" has done well with Pench. I have never heard of this reserve before, but I meant to visit it of course to get information.

August 20th, 2019

RANTHAMBORE NATIONAL PARK

AUG 20

More news on the increase of tiger numbers in India

POSTED 20TH AUGUST 2019

India now has more than 75 per cent of the globe's tigers trotting in the wild. The feel-good is justified as the national animal is faring well in most of the tiger range states despite several odds. Appreciably, the Management Effectiveness Evaluation, a global methodology to assess the functional efficiency of conservation efforts, has rated Pe... ...dia along with Pench Tiger Reserve in Madhya Pradesh.

ANIMAL POACHING
"IS ILLEGAL"

he past 18 years 124 tigers have been poached every

22ND AUGUST 2019

verage, 60 seizures were recorded annually, which means body parts from almost 124 tigers
zed each year. The top three countries with the highest number of seizure incidents were India
10.5 per cent of total seizures), China (126 or 11.0 per cent) and Indonesia (119 or 10.5 per
This was followed by Indonesia and China. At least 259 people were reported to be
argely in China, Indonesia and India. For 17.4 per cent of ...

Yes! I have started to increase my productivity lately. My friend and teachers constantly suggest these websites where I CAN FIND MORE ARTICLES, WITHOUT THE NEED FOR TO RUN AFTER NEWSPAPERS! Yes but anyway, getting to the point, this article sadly isn't one that is surprising. Poaching has been constant and 124 tigers have died in more than 10 years! Seizures incidents have been in 3 countries, India, China and Indonesia. But this isn't good as I feel like even more poaching should be stoppd! And it is still done, people must look into this. There have also been many reports on this and looking more into this topic I feel that more laws and rules should be made to decrease seizure or poaching incidents and decreased instead help increase the tiger population!

August 22nd, 2019

It is September, nice weather outside. But this piece of treasure that I found is extremely interesting. Also EXAMS ARE SO BAD UGH I WISH I COULD HAVE HOLIDAYS AGAIN! But, this is a serious article so I need to focus. There is a reserve in Jharkhand where my mom grew up and they are cutting down trees and this affects tigers! Jharkhand only has one reserve and they are cutting trees to make a "dam". Really people, a dam? I don't know or have studied the importance of that yet but, I, AM NAYONA WOULD SAY "DAMN" TO THIS NEWS. It is sad that the government is actually allowing to happen like come on! I know im just a kid in 7th grade writing this small dumb a entries but this can affect the tiger's habitat! (Also I'm having fun in 7th Grade ha ha)

September 14th, 2019

SEP 14

Almost 350 thousand trees to be lost in Jharkhand's tiger reserve

POSTED 14TH SEPTEMBER 2019

Sadly approval has been granted for thousands of trees to be cut down in Jharkhand's only tiger reserve to make way for a new dam to be created. Parts of Palamau tiger reserve will be lost by this wanton destruction of precious ... resides. ... report can

SAVE THE PLANET

OCT 26

Hopes increase for another Tiger reserve in Rajasthan

POSTED 26TH OCTOBER 2019

A final proposal has been submitted to chief wildlife warden for the same. Following the state government's direction, assessment report on the potential for relocation of the big cats at the sanctuary was prepared by the department. Five tigers, including two males and three females, might be brought to the reserve and they could possibly breed because of which population of 20 tigers can be achieved in a period of 10 years. More on this encouraging report can be seen by foll ...

· HAPPY HALLOWEEN

HALLOWEEN is so close! It's my favourite festival and I can't wait to dress up and go play with my best friend Gayatri! (Still thinking of what to dress up as) but HEY, I also just noticed that I have been writing in this amazing diary FOR MORE THAN A YEAR WOOOOO. This day really is a good day! You know whats even better, the fact that my own classmate helped me find this awesome article on tigers. And today's news is even better, "Hopes increase for another Tiger Reserve in Rajasthan". This includes tigers being transported to reserves to increase the population! There are two males and three females. And im glad that the government is now taking these steps, after the Jharkhand incident* I was worried. But now it's getting better. But I wonder how they would transport the tigers? That must be interesting.

October 26th, 2019

Well it has been almost three months since I have been writing. Yes, I know it was a long time but many many things have been popping up lately. But as a consequence, I read that tigers are in danger again. This is now impacting the Sundarbans and THEY MIGHT BECOME EXTINCT which is definetly not a good thing. This is not only because of us humans but also because of other natural causes such as the climate and rising sea levels. But the other reasons such as loss of habitat, population, prey and more are the reasons that I and many people have already predicted that it would happen. Everyone gets effected by this, not only tigers. But I hope the harm doesn't cause extinction of the Sundarbans as they are a great kind of species and it would of so course be a great loss to the country.

December 19th, 2019

Sundarban and the dangers to its existence

POSTED 19TH DECEMBER 2019

Considering the above fact, it may be pointed out that tigers are getting a double whammy — greater human encroachment on the one hand and a worsening climate and associated sea-level rises on the other. At present, management of tigers is a response to global conservation crisis. Range contraction, population decline, habitat fragmentation, prey loss, and poaching cause and aggravate this crisis. More on this well written article can be seen by following the link below.

SOS

SAVE THE EARTH

Ranthambhore's well known tiger passes away.

POSTED 20TH JANUARY 2020

A famous male tiger named Zalim T25 was found dead in Ranthambore National Park, Rajasthan. He was the same tiger who reared two small orphan cubs. Hindustan TimesZalim will continue to be remembered for a rather heartwarming and rare act that he did - that of rearing orphan twin cubs of T-5 tigress who died in 2011. The two female cubs - around three-months-old at that time - named Bina and Bina-2 were 'adopted by Zalim who kept all other animals away from them. Without ...

Im back from my New Year and Christmas break and 2020 is here! It's a fresh and brand new year. I even got to celebrate my birthday and I'M NOW 12 YEAR OLD WOOOOOO!!! (Sadly don't have pictures this time). But after all the fun and celebration I did, it has come to my notice that a very important tiger has passed. Zalim T25, if those of you that don't know, he gained his popularity by going against the law of nature. It is the original nature of a male tiger to be born and kill or attack their cubs at sight. The male never looks after the cubs, and the female does instead. But Zalim, after the passing of the mother of his their cubs, took care of them, raised them and taught them to hunt! This news a phenomenal was sad but I hope the great tiger rests in peace ♡

January 20ᵗʰ, 2020

Well it has been a while since I have written because of school work and all. Grade 7 is really close to an end and I have been with my friends a lot and have been hanging out. But because of my boredom, I so searched high and low for an article and I got this article which I can only understand a little..... because of my small brain. There has been a concern for tigers from canine distemper. I think my from my understanding it is about dogs probably attacking the tigers or showing threats as they seem to be living in areas really close to the tiger's habitat. They are also being tested as well. Well besides this news, there have been news of the increase of population in tigers which is indeed a good sign. In India especially. It is good news for India but this canine issue is a part of Malaysia.

March 10th, 2020

MAR
10

Concern for tigers from canine distemper

POSTED 10TH MARCH 2020

WWF-Malaysia Tiger Landscape Lead Dr Mark Rayan Darmaraj told the that in the case of an outbreak, dogs living in close proximity to the forest fringes, particularly in villages, plantations and logging camps, could be tested for the presence of CDV antibodies and vaccinated if the tests came back positive. ...

♥SUPPORT♥

Apparently something miserable has happened. Let me explain. Coronavirus has taken over the world and the reason was because of some bats or malfunction in China which is really suspicious. Nevertheless it has been all over the news and it has been said to be an extremely contagious and deadly disease. It can take lives and speed the death toll very quickly. And due to this "pandemic" which is now A GLOBAL CRISIS, the government has imposed a "lockdown." That means... I can't step outside my house, I can't meet my friends or go to school, I have to wear masks all the time and sooner than later my life will have be run by a computer all digitally. Our school and all schools in the world has imposed online or virtual school where I can take my classes from

home through a screen. Hearing all this happening and knowing that normal lifestyle I have is going to change, is scary and at the same time depressing because HOW CAN I STAY IN ONE HOUSE FOR WHO KNOWS HOW LONG. Sorry for ranting but as this is my diary it is best to record such misery. It was said that things would be fine after a week, but I think my life will be like this for another 2 years. It is sad as that means that I will have to graduate 7th Grade virtually and continue 8th Grade and even high school ONLINE. "Not to mention, "puberty", "adolescence" all these words that happen at my age. I'll be facing that nuisance of growing up in a global pandemic. SWEET! I'm so not ready to be a teenager. But as you know how this corona situation is affecting humans, let's see what's affecting the tigers in this!

April 8th, 2020

Acknowledgements

My teachers in Bluebells School International, Maám Bhavana Bhasin (Academic Supervisor – Senior, Bluebells School International), Maám Sohinee Basak and Maám Suman Kumar (Director, Bluebells School International) for encouraging me from the very beginning of this journey. This achievement would not have been possible without your collective encouragement. As this book finds its way into the world, please accept my sincere gratitude for being part of this transformative chapter.

CBSE Board, the opportunities I found whilst doing Project Tiger, inspired this book.

The newspapers and websites in my bibliography for their inspiring and articulate reporting and articles which I would read in my school library and cut-out for my diary inputs.

Sameer, Shruti and the team at BlueRose Publishers, for helping to bring this book to life – this is just the beginning!

Mom, Dad, my two remarkable Grannies, Richa (my sister), Abhijay and Ruhaan (my brothers), Anneka and my family for always having my back. I'm here because of your relentless support and belief in me.

My friends, for being the best sounding boards and for being there for me always.

A big thank you to designer Anushka Tandon for the amazing book design.

Bibliography

1. https://phys.org/news/2018-11-rare-sumatran-tiger-beneath-indonesia.html

2. https://www.seattletimes.com/nation-world/aww-times-4-berlin-zoo-fetes-birth-of-sumatran-tiger-cubs/

3. https://m.timesofindia.com/home/environment/flora-fauna/royal-bengal-tigers-spotted-in-three-new-locations-in-odisha/articleshow/66013104.cms?frmapp=yes

4. https://timesofindia.indiatimes.com/city/pune/maha-loses-16-tigers-in-11-months/articleshow/66790022.cms

5. https://timesofindia.indiatimes.com/city/bhubaneswar/satkosia-littered-with-metal-snares/articleshow/66671461.cms

6. https://timesofindia.indiatimes.com/city/nagpur/reinforce-rules-in-tiger-corridors-buffer-zones-ntca/articleshow/66871964.cms

7. https://toistudent.timesofindia.indiatimes.com/news/top-news/learning-with-times-nie-what-are-tigon-and-liger/42174.html#:~:text=Nat%20Geo%20Uncle%3A%20A%20Tigon,a%20female%20tiger(tigress).

8. https://www.hindustantimes.com/world-news/climate-change-could-wipe-out-bengal-tigers-over-next-50-years-scientists/story-QeU5Lb9aGDsBtXjbGMbOWJ.html

9. https://indianexpress.com/article/explained/explained-reasons-to-cheer-the-birth-of-amur-tiger-cubs-in-dublin-zoo-5558126/#:~:text=The%20Amur%20tiger%20cubs%20that,mother%20Tundra%20on%20October%2014.

10. https://www.deccanherald.com/science/tiger-tiger-burning-bright-735940.html

11. https://www.newindianexpress.com/thesundaystandard/2019/may/26/tiger-spotting-in-the-heart-of-corbett-1981906.html

12. https://www.livemint.com/news/india/tiger-count-rises-33-in-india-but-the-roar-is-uneven-across-states-1564384170129.html

13. https://www.hindustantimes.com/ranchi/over-3-44-lakh-trees-to-be-cut-in-jharkhand-s-palamau-tiger-reserve/story-c1ldPUezEqw6VemMOGygsK.html

14. https://www.tigersintheforest.co.uk/articles/hopes-increase-for-another-tiger-reserve-in-rajasthan

15. https://www.tigersintheforest.co.uk/articles/sundarban-and-the-dangers-to-its-existence

16. https://indianexpress.com/article/india/ranthambore-tiger-that-adopted-and-reared-two-cubs-found-dead-6227039/

17. https://www.tigersintheforest.co.uk/articles/concern-for-tigers-from-canine-distemper